HEINEMANN MODULAR MAT
for
EDEXCEL AS AND A-LEVEL
Revise for
Decision Maths 1

John Hebborn

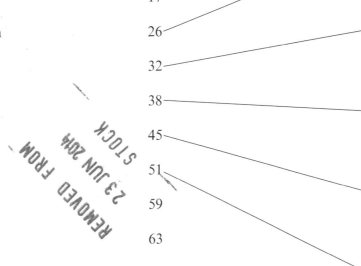

Heinemann

Edexcel
Success through qualifications

Heinemann Educational Publishers,
Halley Court, Jordan Hill, Oxford OX2 8EJ
Part of Harcourt Education

Heinemann is the registered trademark of Harcourt Education Limited

First Published 2001

05   04   03
10   9   8   7   6   5   4

ISBN 0 435 51119 X

Cover design by Gecko Limited

Original design by Geoffrey Wadsley; additional design work by Jim Turner

Typeset and illustrated by Tech-Set Limited, Gateshead, Tyne and Wear

Printed and bound in the UK by Scotprint

Acknowledgements

The publisher's and authors' thanks are due to Edexcel for permission to
reproduce questions from past examination papers. These are marked with an [E].

The answers have been provided by the authors and are not the responsibility
of the examining board.

About this book

This book is designed to help you get your best possible grade in your Decision Maths 1 examination. The series authors are Chief and Principal examiners and moderators, and have a good understanding of Edexcel's requirements.

Revise for Decision Maths 1 covers the key topics that are tested in the Decision Maths 1 exam paper. You can use this book to help you revise at the end of your course, or you can use it throughout your course alongside the course textbook; *Heinemann Modular Mathematics for Edexcel AS and A-level Decision Mathematics 1*, which provides complete coverage of the syllabus.

Helping you prepare for your exam

To help you prepare, each topic offers you:

- **Key points to remember** – summarise the mathematical ideas you need to know and be able to use.
- **Worked examples and examination questions** – help you understand and remember important methods, and show you how to set out your answers clearly.
- **Revision exercises** – help you practise using these important methods to solve problems. Past paper questions are included so you can be sure you are reaching the right standard, and answers are given at the back of the book so you can assess your progress.
- **Test yourself questions** – help you see where you need extra revision and practice. If you do need extra help they show you where to look in the *Heinemann Modular Mathematics for Edexcel AS and A-level Decision Mathematics 1* textbook.

Exam practice and advice on revising

Examination style practice paper – this paper at the end of the book provides a set of questions of examination standard. It gives you an opportunity to practise taking a complete exam before you meet the real thing. The answers are given at the back of the book.

How to revise – for advice on revising before the exam, read the How to revise section on the next page.

How to revise using this book

Making the best use of your revision time

The topics in this book have been arranged in a logical sequence so you can work your way through them from beginning to end. But **how** you work on them depends on how much time there is between now and your examination.

If you have plenty of time before the exam then you can **work through each topic in turn**, covering the key points and worked examples before doing the revision exercises and test yourself questions.

If you are short of time then you can **work through the Test yourself sections** first, to help you see which topics you need to do further work on.

However much time you have to revise, make sure you break your revision into short blocks of about 40 minutes, separated by five- or ten-minute breaks. Nobody can study effectively for hours without a break.

Using the Test yourself sections

Each Test yourself section provides a set of key questions. Try each question:

- If you can do it and get the correct answer then move on to the next topic. Come back to this topic later to consolidate your knowledge and understanding by working through the key points, worked examples and revision exercises.

- If you cannot do the question, or get an incorrect answer or part answer, then work through the key points, worked examples and revision exercises before trying the Test yourself questions again. If you need more help, the cross-references beside each test yourself question show you where to find relevant information in the *Heinemann Modular Mathematics for Edexcel AS and A-level Decision Mathematics 1* textbook.

Reviewing the key points

Most of the key points are straightforward ideas that you can learn: try to understand each one. Imagine explaining each idea to a friend in your own words, and say it out loud as you do so. This is a better way of making the ideas stick than just reading them silently from the page.

As you work through the book, remember to go back over key points from earlier topics at least once a week. This will help you to remember them in the exam.

Algorithms

1

Key points to remember

1 An **algorithm** is a set of precise instructions which if followed will solve a problem.

2 **The bubble-sort algorithm**
To sort a list compare adjacent members of the list, moving from left to right, and switch them if they are in the wrong order. Continue this process until a pass produces no change in the list.

3 **The quick-sort algorithm**
  Step 1 Select a specific number (the pivot) from the list, say the middle one.
  Step 2 Write all numbers smaller than the pivot to the left of the pivot, reading the original list from left to right, and so create a sublist L_1.
  Write all numbers larger than the pivot to the right of the pivot, reading the original list from left to right, and so create a sublist L_2.
  Step 3 Apply step 1 and step 2 to each sublist until all the sublists contain only one number.

4 **First-fit algorithm**
Taking the boxes in the order listed place the next box to be packed in the *first* available bin that can take that box.

5 **First-fit decreasing algorithm**
  Step 1 Reorder the boxes in *decreasing* order of size.
  Step 2 Apply the first-fit algorithm to the reordered list.

6 **Binary-search algorithm**
May be applied to search a list of names in alphabetical order or a list of numbers in ascending order.
  Step 1 Compare the required item with the middle item in the list. If this is the required item then the search is complete.
    (i) If the required item is before the middle item then consider the top half of the list.
    (ii) If the required item is after the middle item then consider the bottom half of the list.

| **Step 2** | Apply step 1 to the top half of the list in case (i) or the bottom half of the list in case (ii). |
| **Stop** | Either when the required item is located or when it has been shown that the required item is not in the list. |

Example 1

Use the flowchart shown opposite to determine if 79 is a prime number.

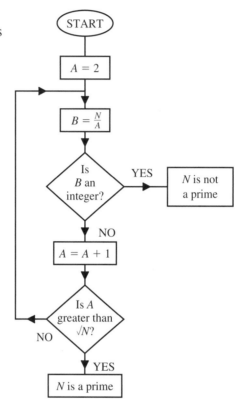

Answer

The results of applying the algorithm are shown in the table below. (Using a calculator $\sqrt{79} = 8.89$ to 3 s.f.)

A	$B = \dfrac{79}{A}$	B an integer?	$A + 1$	$> \sqrt{79}$
2	39.5	No	3	No
3	26.3	No	4	No
4	19.8	No	5	No
5	15.8	No	6	No
6	13.2	No	7	No
7	11.3	No	8	No
8	9.88	No	9	Yes

Hence we have shown that 79 is a prime. You will often be given a table of the above kind to complete in the examination. If you are not given a table you should consider if the production of such a table will save you a lot of writing. In this example the use of a table does just this.

Example 2

The following algorithm obtains the solution of the quadratic equation $ax^2 + bx + c = 0$, $a \neq 0$.

Step 1 Divide the equation by the coefficient of x^2.

Step 2 Subtract the constant term from both sides of the equation.

Step 3 Find half the coefficient of x, square it and add it to both sides of the equation.

Step 4 Rewrite the left-hand side of the equation as a perfect square.

Step 5 Take the square root of both sides of the equation.

Step 6 Solve for x.

> The coefficient of x^2 is the number a.

Use this algorithm to solve the equation $3x^2 + 11x + 10 = 0$.

Answer

Step 1 $x^2 + \dfrac{11}{3}x + \dfrac{10}{3} = 0$

Step 2 $x^2 + \dfrac{11}{3}x = -\dfrac{10}{3}$

Step 3 $x^2 + \dfrac{11}{3}x + \left(\dfrac{11}{6}\right)^2 = -\dfrac{10}{3} + \left(\dfrac{11}{6}\right)^2 = \dfrac{-120 + 121}{36}$

$$= \dfrac{1}{36}$$

Step 4 $\left(x + \dfrac{11}{6}\right)^2 = \dfrac{1}{36}$

Step 5 $x + \dfrac{11}{6} = \pm\dfrac{1}{6}$ (Don't forget there are two square roots.)

Step 6 $x = -\dfrac{11}{6} \pm \dfrac{1}{6}$

So $x = -\dfrac{11}{6} + \dfrac{1}{6} = -\dfrac{10}{6} = -\dfrac{5}{3}$

or $x = -\dfrac{11}{6} - \dfrac{1}{6} = -\dfrac{12}{6} = -2$

Example 3

$$45, \quad 33, \quad 76, \quad 88, \quad 52, \quad 64$$

Sort the above list into decreasing order using
(a) the bubble-sort algorithm,
(b) the quick-sort algorithm.

Answer

(a) Using **2**, the bubble-sort algorithm, the first pass is:

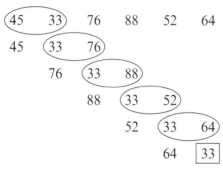

At the end of the second pass we obtain:

$$76 \quad 88 \quad 52 \quad 64 \quad \boxed{45} \quad \boxed{33}$$

At the end of the third pass we obtain:

$$88 \quad 76 \quad 64 \quad \boxed{52} \quad \boxed{45} \quad \boxed{33}$$

At the end of the fourth pass we obtain:

$$88 \quad 76 \quad 64 \quad 52 \quad 45 \quad 33$$

Since there are no changes from the previous list this is the final list with numbers in decreasing order.

(b) Using **3**, we take the 'middle' number 88 as the pivot to obtain:

$$\boxed{88} \quad 45 \quad 33 \quad 76 \quad 52 \quad 64$$

At the next stage we obtain:

$$\boxed{88} \quad \boxed{76} \quad 45 \quad 33 \quad 52 \quad 64$$

The remaining stages are:

$$\boxed{88} \quad \boxed{76} \quad 64 \quad \boxed{52} \quad 45 \quad 33$$

and

$$\boxed{88} \quad \boxed{76} \quad \boxed{64} \quad \boxed{52} \quad 45 \quad \boxed{33}$$

and

$$\boxed{88} \quad \boxed{76} \quad \boxed{64} \quad \boxed{52} \quad \boxed{45} \quad \boxed{33}$$

The sorting is now complete. At each stage the 'middle' number was chosen as the pivot.

> You should always carry out this step.

Example 4

Use the binary-search algorithm to locate the name M O N K in the following list:

1 A B L E
2 B R O W N
3 C O X
4 D E N Y E R
5 F I D D L E R
6 G R A N D
7 M O N K
8 P E P P E R
9 R I C H

Answer

The middle name in the list is F I D D L E R. As M O N K is after this we consider the reduced list:

6 G R A N D
7 M O N K
8 P E P P E R
9 R I C H

The middle name in this reduced list is P E P P E R.
If M O N K is in the list it will occur before P E P P E R and so we consider the reduced list:

6 G R A N D
7 M O N K

The middle name in this list is M O N K and so we have located the given name at position 7.

Example 5

A project is to be completed in 16 hours. The activities involved in the project and their duration in hours are given in the table below.

A	B	C	D	E	F	G	H
3	5	8	5	4	9	8	5

To determine how many workers are required:
(a) apply the first-fit algorithm
(b) apply the first-fit decreasing algorithm.
Is it possible to obtain a better solution than either (a) or (b)?

Answer

(a) Application of the first-fit algorithm gives:

Using ▪4

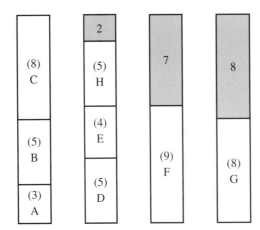

Four workers are required.

(b) Ordering the durations in decreasing order we obtain:

This is step 1 of ▪5

9	8	8	5	5	5	4	3
F	C	G	B	D	H	E	A

Applying the first-fit algorithm to this list gives:

Using ▪4

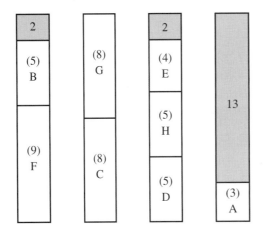

Again four workers are required.

This arrangement only uses three workers:

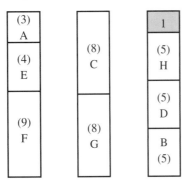

Revision exercise 1

1 Use the Euclidean algorithm given by the flowchart below to find the highest common factor of 27 and 153.

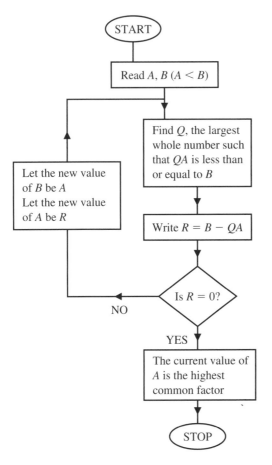

2 To solve the simultaneous equations

$$ax + by = c \quad \text{(i)}$$
$$Ax + By = C \quad \text{(ii)} \quad (Ab - Ba \neq 0)$$

Step 1 Multiply equation (i) by A to give equation (iii).

Step 2 Multiply equation (ii) by a to give equation (iv).

Step 3 Subtract equation (iv) from equation (iii).

Step 4 Solve resulting equation for y.

Step 5 Substitute the value of y found into equation (i) to obtain x.

Use this algorithm to solve the simultaneous equations

$$6x - 5y = 8$$
$$5x + y = 17$$

3 The weights of the edges of a connected graph are, in centimetres:

$$38, \quad 24, \quad 46, \quad 63, \quad 57, \quad 30$$

In order to use Kruskal's algorithm we require the weights of the edges to be sorted into increasing order. Obtain the required order using:

(a) the bubble-sort algorithm

(b) the quick-sort algorithm.

4 Kate wishes to record several TV programmes on 2-hour tapes. The lengths of the programmes are:

20 min, 40 min, 1 hour 20 min, 30 min, 1 hour 10 min, 30 min, 1 hour 30 min.

Help Kate to decide how many 2-hour tapes she requires using:

(a) the first-fit algorithm

(b) the first-fit decreasing algorithm.

5 Use the binary-search algorithm to locate the name LION in the following alphabetical list:

1 ABBOTT	2 BRIGHT	3 CROWN
4 GILBERT	5 JONES	6 LION
7 MUSGROVE	8 NEIL	9 SIDNEY

Test yourself	**What to review**

If your answer is incorrect:

1 In this question f(a) is the value of the function f(x) when $x = a$. For example, if f(x) = $x^2 + 6x - 72$ then f(2) = $(2)^2 + 6(2) - 72 = -56$
The bisection algorithm is given below.
Step 1 Set $L = 0$, $U = 16$
Step 2 Let $FL = $ f(L) and $FU = $ f(U).
Step 3 Let $M = \frac{1}{2}(L + U)$
Step 4 Let $FM = $ f(M)
Step 5 If $FM < 0$ then let $L = M$ and $FL = FM$ and return to step 3.
Step 6 If $FM > 0$ then let $U = M$ and $FU = FM$ and return to step 3.
Step 7 If $FM = 0$ then stop.
Apply this algorithm to the function f(x) = $x^2 + 6x - 72$. You should write down your final value of M. What is the significance of this value?

Review Heinemann Book D1 pages 1–7

2 BULL, GOUGH, HUNT, AHMED, DODGE, ELDER, NOON.

(a) Use the quick-sort algorithm to sort the above list of names into alphabetical order.

(b) Use the binary-search algorithm to confirm that the name GOOD is not in the list.

Review Heinemann Book D1 pages 10–12, 21–24

---

3 (a) Use the bubble-sort algorithm to sort the list 4, 6, 7, 8, 5 into descending order.

(b) Paul is making a model and requires the following lengths of balsa wood:

$$8\,\text{cm}, 4\,\text{cm}, 6\,\text{cm}, 7\,\text{cm}, 8\,\text{cm}, 5\,\text{cm}, 7\,\text{cm}$$

The wood comes in 15 cm lengths.
Use the first-fit decreasing algorithm to obtain the number of lengths required.

Review Heinemann Book D1 pages 7–10, 16–19

Test yourself answers

1 $M = 6$, $f(6) = 0$, therefore $x = 6$ is a solution of $f(x) = 0$

2 (a) AHMED, BULL, DODGE, ELDER, GOUGH, HUNT, NOON

3 (a) 8, 7, 6, 5, 4 **(b)** Three lengths are required

Graphs and networks

This chapter is important because it contains many of the definitions of graph theory, which are employed in the chapters that follow. You should make sure that you are very familiar with the following definitions:

Key points to remember

1 A **graph** *G* consists of a finite number of points (usually called vertices or nodes) connected by lines (usually called edges or arcs).

2 A **path** is a finite sequence of edges such that the end vertex of one edge in the sequence is the start vertex of the next, and in which no vertex appears more than once.

3 A **cycle** (or circuit) is a closed path, i.e. the end vertex of the last edge is the start vertex of the first edge.

4 A **Hamiltonian cycle** is a cycle that passes through every vertex of the graph once and only once, and returns to its start vertex.

5 A **Eulerian cycle** is a cycle that includes every edge of a graph exactly once.

> Whenever it appears in the exam 'Eulerian cycle' will be defined.

6 The **vertex set** is the set of all vertices of a graph.

7 The **edge set** is the set of all edges of a graph.

8 A **subgraph** of a graph is a subset of the vertices together with a subset of edges.

9 Two vertices are **connected** if there is a path between them.

10 A graph is **connected** if all pairs of its vertices are connected

11 A **simple graph** is one in which there is no edge with the same vertex at each end, i.e. no loops, and not more than one edge connecting any pair of vertices.

12 The **degree** (or valency or order) of a vertex is the number of edges connected to it.

13 If the edges of a graph have a direction associated with them they are known as **directed edges**, and the graph is known as a **digraph**.

14 A **tree** is a connected graph with no cycles.

15 A **spanning tree** of a graph G is a subgraph that includes all the vertices of G and is also a tree.

16 A **bipartite graph** consists of two set of vertices, X and Y. The edges only join vertices in X to vertices in Y, not vertices within a set.

17 If there are r vertices in X and s vertices in Y and every vertex in X is joined to every vertex in Y then the graph is called $K_{r,s}$.

18 A graph in which each of the n vertices is connected to every other vertex is called a **complete graph**, K_n.

Example 1

Four boys, Albert (A), Bill (B), Colin (C) and David (D) were asked which of four swimming events, breaststroke (1), backstroke (2), butterfly (3) or freestyle (4), they were willing to take part in. Their replies are summarised in the table below.

A	2, 3 4
B	1, 4
C	2, 3
D	1, 2, 4

Represent (model) this information as a bipartite graph.

Using **16**

Answer

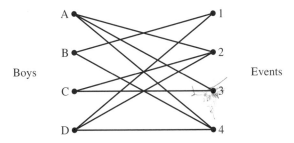

Boys and events are represented by vertices. Edges indicate the willingness of a boy to take part in that event.

Example 2

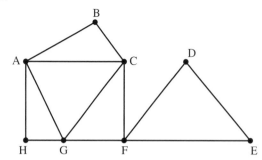

(a) Write down the degree (valency) of each vertex in the above graph.

| Using 12 |

(b) Obtain an Eulerian cycle for the graph.

| Using 5 |

(c) If the edge *AC* is removed is it still possible to obtain a Eulerian cycle?

Answer

(a) The degrees (valencies) of each vertex are:

| Using 12 |

$$A\ (4),\ B\ (2),\ C\ (4),\ D\ (2),\ E\ (2),\ F\ (4),\ G\ (4),\ H\ (2)$$

(b) An Eulerian cycle is a cycle that includes every edge of the graph exactly once.

| Using 5 |

Such a cycle for the given graph is:

$$A\ B\ C\ F\ D\ E\ F\ G\ C\ A\ G\ H\ A$$

(c) No. Vertices A and C now have valency 3, i.e. they are odd vertices and so the graph is not traversable.

Example 3

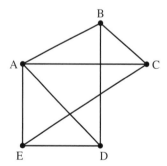

Obtain a Hamiltonian cycle for the above graph, which starts and finishes at A.

| Using 4 |

Answer

Such a cycle is A C B D E A

Example 4

The table below gives the distances, in kilometres, between some towns. Use the information to draw a network.

	A	B	C	D	E
A	0	25	—	30	—
B	25	0	8	18	15
C	—	8	0	6	12
D	30	18	6	0	16
E	—	15	12	16	0

Answer

We start with A, which is only joined to B and D, as we can see from the first line of the table.

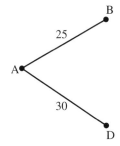

We then notice that D is joined to all the other towns:

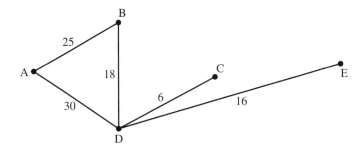

The network may be completed by adding BC, BE and CE:

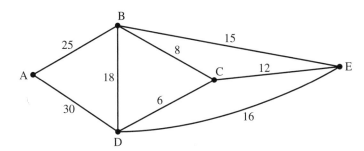

Example 5

Draw **(a)** K_5 (the complete graph on 5 vertices) and **(b)** $K_{4,2}$.
(c) Write down the valencies of the vertices in each case.

Answer

(a) K_5 is the complete graph on five vertices, i.e. each vertex is joined to every other vertex:

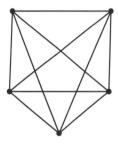

(b) $K_{4,2}$ is the bipartite graph with four vertices in one set and two vertices in the other set:

Using **17**

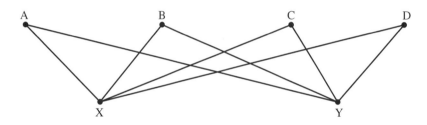

(c) In K_5 each vertex has valency 4.
In $K_{4,2}$ two vertices, X and Y, have valency 4 and four vertices, A, B, C and D, have valency 2.

Revision exercise 2

1 For the bipartite graph shown in Example 1 obtain a Hamiltonian cycle.

2 Starting with vertex A, draw a spanning tree for the graph shown in Example 1.

3 Obtain the distance matrix for the network shown below.

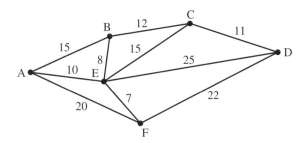

4 Find all possible routes from A to E in the directed network shown below.

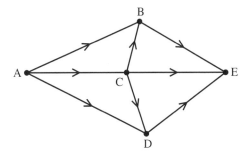

5 Is it possible to find a Eulerian cycle for the graph shown in Example 1? Give a reason for your answer.

6

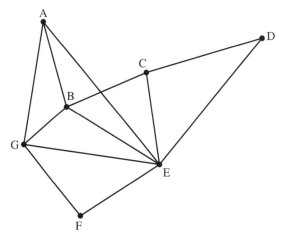

It is not possible to obtain a Eulerian cycle for the graph above. By adding one further edge it is possible to obtain a graph that does have a Eulerian cycle. State the edge that should be added and explain why the resulting graph has a Eulerian cycle. Write down this cycle.

Test yourself | What to review

If your answer is incorrect:

Review Heinemann Book D1 pages 27–48

1

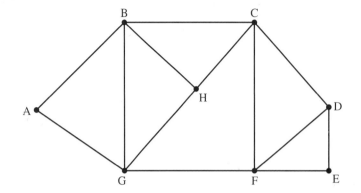

For the above graph:
(a) draw a spanning tree, starting with vertex A
(b) write down a Hamiltonian cycle for the graph starting at A
(c) write down the valencies of the vertices.

Using your answer to (c) show that, by inserting a further edge, it is possible to make the graph Eulerian. State this edge and give a possible Eulerian cycle in the augmented graph.

Test yourself answers

1 (a) e.g.

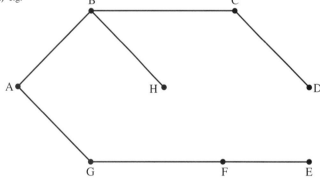

(b) ABHCDEFGA   **(c)** A(2), B(4), C(4), D(3), E(2), F(4), G(4), H(3)

Add edge DH – this makes all vertices even and the augmented graph Eulerian. ABCDEFDHCFGHBGA.

Algorithms on graphs

3

Key points to remember

1 A **minimum spanning tree** of a connected and undirected graph is a spanning tree such that the total length of its edges is as small as possible. (This is sometimes called a minimum connector.)

2 **Kruskal's algorithm** builds a minimum spanning tree by adding one **edge** at a time to a subgraph. At each stage the edge of smallest weight is chosen provided that it does not create a cycle with edges already chosen.

3 **Prim's algorithm** builds a minimum spanning tree by adding one **vertex** at a time to a connected subgraph. The new vertex to be added is the one that is nearest to **any** vertex already in the subgraph.

4 **Dijkstra's algorithm** obtains the shortest route from the initial vertex to any other vertex in a network. At each stage a fresh vertex is assigned a **final label** that gives the shortest distance from the initial vertex to that vertex.

5 A **planar graph** is a graph that can be drawn in a plane in such a way that no two edges meet each other, except at a vertex to which they are both incident.

6 The **planarity algorithm** can only be applied to graphs that have a Hamiltonian circuit.

Example 1

The diagram on the next page shows locations A, B, C, ..., J in a theme park and the paths connecting them. The lengths of the paths are given in kilometres.

(a) Use Dijkstra's algorithm to find the shortest route from A to J. It is planned that all the locations will be connected by a telephone system with the cables laid alongside the paths. The operating company wishes to use a minimum length of cable.

(b) Use Kruskal's algorithm to obtain a minimum spanning tree and hence find this minimum length.

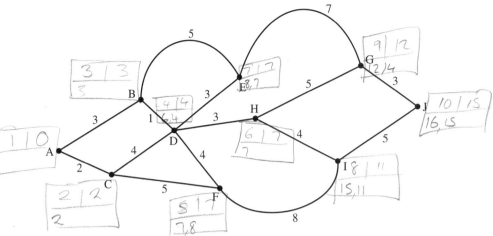

(c) Use Prim's algorithm to obtain a minimum spanning tree and hence find this minimum length.

(d) Use the information in the network to construct a distance matrix. Use Prim's algorithm on this matrix to verify your answer to (c).

Answer

(a) The figure below shows the result of applying Dijkstra's algorithm.

Using ▣ 4

The key is:

Location	Order of labelling	Final value
Working values		

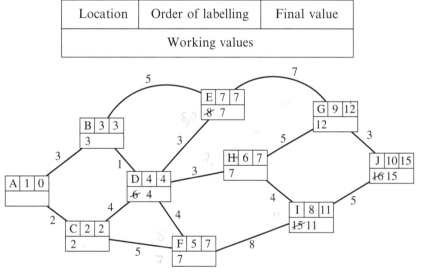

The length of the shortest route from A to J is given by the final value for J, namely 15 km.

To obtain the shortest route we work backwards from J:

final value J – final value G = 15–12 = length GJ (3)
final value G – final value H = 12–7 = length HG (5)
final value H – final value D = 7–4 = length DH (3)
final value D – final value B = 4–3 = length BD (1)
final value B – final value A = 3–0 = length AB (3)

Hence the shortest route is ABDHGJ.

(b) To use Kruskal's algorithm we need to order the edges in increasing order of their weight.
This order is:

BD (1), AC (2), AB (3), DH (3), DE (3), GJ (3), CD (4), DF (4), HI (4), CF (5), BE (5), HG (5), IJ (5), EG (7), FI (8)

All edges of weights 1, 2 and 3 may be chosen without forming any cycles.
The edge CD (4) cannot be chosen as its choice would create a cycle.
The edges DF (4) and HI (4) may be chosen.
The edges CF (5) and BE (5) cannot be chosen as their choice would create cycles.
The edge HG can be chosen.
All vertices are now connected and the minimum spanning tree is

Using **2**

Using **2**

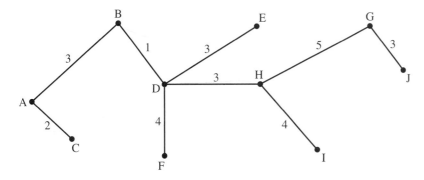

Weight is 28, therefore the minimum length of cable is 28 km.
(c) Start with vertex A. The vertices, using Prim's algorithm, are added in the order shown below using the edges indicated:

Using **3**

A, C (AC), B (AB), D (BD), E (DE), H (DH), F (DF), I (HI), G (HG), J (GJ)

The minimum spanning tree obtained is

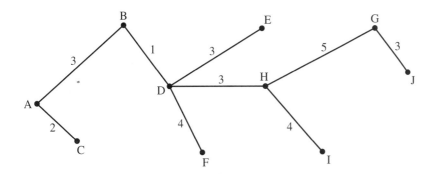

The total weight is 28 and so the minimum length of cable is 28 km.

(d) The distance matrix for the network given is:

	A	B	C	D	E	F	G	H	I	J
A	—	3	2	—	—	—	—	—	—	—
B	3	—	—	1	5	—	—	—	—	—
C	2	—	—	4	—	5	—	—	—	—
D	—	1	4	—	3	4	—	3	—	—
E	—	5	—	3	—	—	7	—	—	—
F	—	—	5	4	—	—	—	—	8	—
G	—	—	—	—	7	—	—	5	—	3
H	—	—	—	3	—	—	5	—	4	—
I	—	—	—	—	—	8	—	4	—	5
J	—	—	—	—	—	—	3	—	5	—

Applying Prim's algorithm to this distance matrix produces the result below, where the circles denote the edges in the minimum spanning tree and the numbers above the vertices give the order in which the vertices were added.

Using **5**

	1	3	2	4	5	7	9	6	8	10
	A	B	C	D	E	F	G	H	I	J
A	—	3	2	—	—	—	—	—	—	—
B	③	—	—	1	5	—	—	—	—	—
C	②	—	—	4	—	5	—	—	—	—
D	—	①	4	—	3	4	—	3	—	—
E	—	5	—	③	—	—	7	—	—	—
F	—	—	5	④	—	—	—	—	8	—
G	—	—	—	—	7	—	—	⑤	—	3
H	—	—	—	③	—	—	5	—	4	—
I	—	—	—	—	—	8	—	④	—	5
J	—	—	—	—	—	—	③	—	5	—

The minimum spanning tree corresponding to the above result is

Using **1**

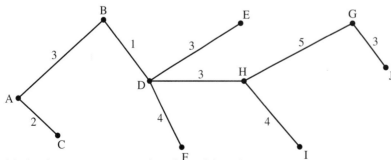

This is the same tree as that found in (c).
There are other minimum spanning trees for this network but they all have a total weight of 28.

Example 2

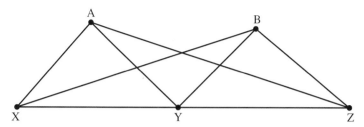

Use the planarity algorithm to show that the graph above is a planar graph.

Answer

We first identify a Hamiltonian circuit in the graph, namely AXBYZA.

Redrawing the graph with the circuit as a polygon we obtain:

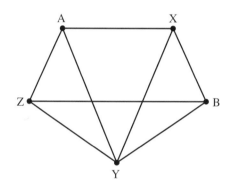

Let edge ZB remain inside the polygon. Moving edges AY and XY outside gives:

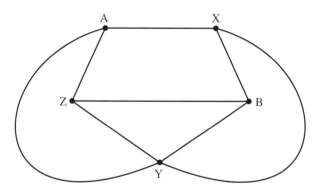

This is a planar graph and so the given graph is planar.

Using **5**

Revision exercise 3

1 Use Kruskal's algorithm to find two minimum spanning trees for the network shown below. Find the total weight of each of these trees.

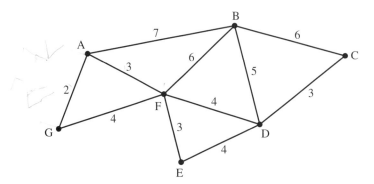

2 A garden centre is planning to install a complete water system connecting all the various plant areas. The locations of the plant areas and the distances, in metres, between them are shown on the network below. The company wishes to find the least amount of pipe that needs to be used. Use Prim's algorithm to find a minimum spanning tree for the network and hence find the minimum length of pipe that will be required.

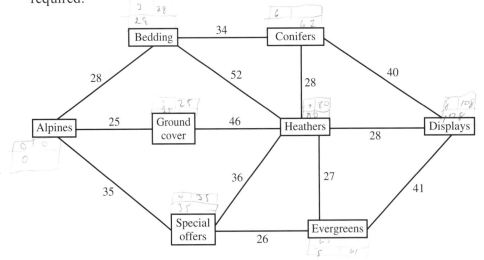

3

	A	B	C	D	E	F	G
A	—	10	12	23	—	—	—
B	10	—	—	18	12	—	—
C	12	—	—	12	—	8	—
D	23	18	12	—	10	10	9
E	—	12	—	10	—	—	13
F	—	—	8	10	—	—	14
G	—	—	—	9	13	14	—

Use Prim's algorithm on the distance matrix above to obtain a minimum spanning tree for the network which models this matrix. Draw the tree and state its total weight.

4

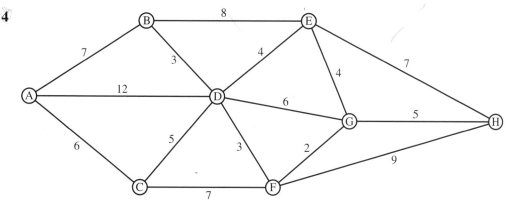

The diagram above shows locations A, B, C, …, H in a country park and the roads connecting them. The distances along the roads are given in miles.

(a) Use Dijkstra's algorithm to find the shortest route from A to H. State the length of the shortest route.

(b) Due to flooding all roads through G are impassable. Find the shortest route from A to H now and state its length.

5 Use the planarity algorithm to show that the graph opposite is planar. Draw a planar representation of this graph.

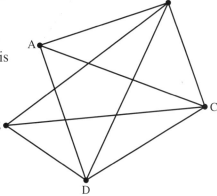

Test yourself

1

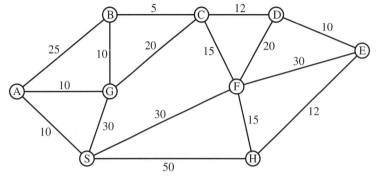

Fiona lives at S and works at E. The network shows the roads in the area that she may use on her journey to work and the time, in minutes, it takes her to traverse these roads. Use Dijkstra's algorithm to obtain the quickest routes from S to E. You should show all your working on a copy of the network and state the time taken to complete the quickest routes. You should also explain carefully how you obtained your quickest routes from your labelling.

Review Heinemann Book D1 pages 63–69

2

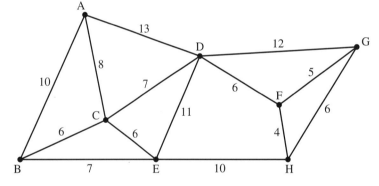

Review Heinemann Book D1 pages 51–60

(a) State briefly:
   (i) Prim's algorithm
   (ii) Kruskal's algorithm.

(b) Find a minimum spanning tree for the network shown above using:
   (i) Prim's algorithm, starting with vertex F
   (ii) Kruskal's algorithm.
In each case write down the order in which you made your selection of arcs.
(c) State the weight of your spanning tree.
(d) State, giving a reason for your answer, which algorithm is preferable for a large network.

3 Use the planarity algorithm to determine if the graph shown below is planar.

Review Heinemann Book D1 pages 72–75

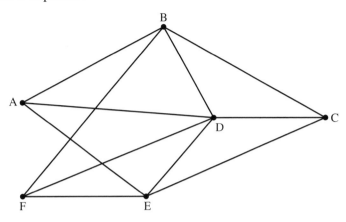

Test yourself answers

1 Labels: S (0), A (10), B (30), C (35), D (47), E (57), F (30), G (20), H (45) Shortest routes are SAGBCDE and SFHE
Time taken to complete quickest route is 57 minutes

2 (b) (i) FH, FG, FD, DC, CB, CE, CA   (ii) FH, FG, FD, CE, CB, CD, CA

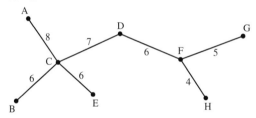

(c) Total weight = 42
(d) Prim – easily programmable for a computer. Checking for cycles in Kruskal is difficult.

3 A Hamiltonian circuit is ADFBCEA

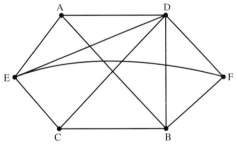

Move DB and AB outside to obtain

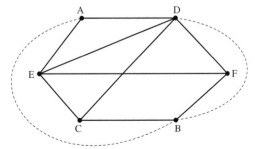

Edge DC cannot be moved so as to remove crossings, hence graph is not planar.

The route inspection problem

4

Key points to remember

1 A **traversable graph** is one that can be drawn without removing your pen from the paper and without going over the same edge twice.

2 If in a graph there is a route that starts and finishes at the same vertex and traverses every edge once and only once then the graph is **Eulerian**.

3 If a graph is not Eulerian but there is a route starting and finishing at different vertices and traversing every edge once and only once then the graph is **semi-Eulerian**.

4 **The handshaking theorem**
The **sum** of the valencies, taken over all vertices of a graph G, is equal to **twice** the number of edges.

5 **The route inspection problem**
In a given undirected network a route of **minimum weight** has to be found that traverses every edge at least once, returning to the starting vertex.

Example 1

Prove that this graph is traversable and write down a route starting at A and returning to A that traverses each edge exactly once.

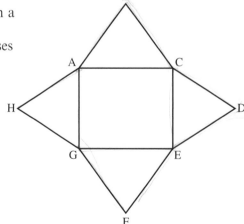

Answer

The valencies (degrees) of the vertices are:

A (4), B (2), C (4), D (2), E (4), F (2), G (4), H (2)

Since all the vertices are even the graph is traversable.
A possible route starting at A is:

Using **1**

ABCDEFGECAGHA

Example 2

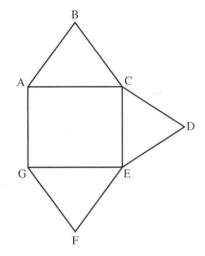

Show that the above graph is not Eulerian but is semi-Eulerian. Write down the possible route and the starting and finishing vertices.

Answer

The valencies of the vertices are:

A (3), B (2), C (4), D (2), E (4), F (2), G (3)

As not all the vertices are even, the graph is not Eulerian. However, there are just two odd vertices, A and G, and there is therefore the possibility that a route, starting at A and finishing at G and traversing each edge exactly once, can be found. Such a route is:

Using **2**

Using **3**

ABCDEFGACEG

Example 3

The villages in a country area, A, B, C, ..., I, are joined by the roads shown with their lengths shown in kilometres.

(a) Solve the route inspection problem for this network, stating clearly which edges are to be repeated. Give a possible route and its length.

(b) A new road HE of length 8 km is built. Obtain the route now and give its length.

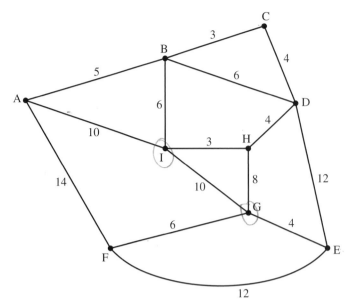

Answer

(a) The odd vertices in this graph are A (3), E (3), F (3) and H (3).
The possible pairings are:
(i)   (A, E) and (F, H)
(ii) (A, F) and (E, H)
(iii) (A, H) and (E, F).
The edges to be repeated and the increased length of the resulting route are:
(i)   (A, E) and (F, H)
      The shortest path between A and E, found by inspection is ABDE, length $= 5 + 6 + 12 = 23$.
      The shortest path between F and H is FGH,
      length $= 6 + 8 = 14$.
      Using this pairing the additional length is $23 + 14 = 37$.
(ii) (A, F) and (E, H)
      The shortest path between A and F is AF, length $= 14$.
      The shortest path between E and H is EGH, length $= 12$.
      Using this paring the additional length is $14 + 12 = 26$.
(iii) (A, H) and (E, F)
      The shortest route between A and H is AIH, length $= 13$.
      The shortest route between E and F is EGF, length $= 10$.
      Using this pairing the additional length is $13 + 10 = 23$.
      Pairing (iii) is the 'best' pairing as 23 is smaller than the 37 and 26 of pairings (i) and (ii).
      If we use pairing (iii) then we must repeat edges AI and IH, and edges EG and GF.
      A possible route is:

A F E G F G E D C B D H G I H I B A I A

Using **5**

The length of this route is:

(Total weight of edges) $+23 = 107 + 23 = 130$

(b) The addition of the edge HE makes both E and H even vertices. The only odd vertices are now A and F. The route now only has to repeat AF.
The total length of route is:

(Total weight of edges) $+ 14 = (107 + 8) + 14 = 129$

This is shorter than the route found in (a).
A possible route is now:

AFEDHEGHIBDCBAIGFA

Revision exercise 4

1

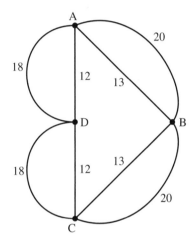

The above diagram shows the paths in a formal garden and their lengths in appropriate units.

(a) Show that the graph is traversable.

(b) Hence obtain a route of minimum length that the gardener could take to check the condition of all the paths. State its length.

2

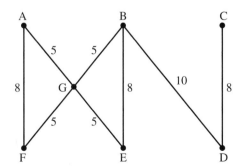

A machinist wishes to sew the above symbol onto a cloth.
The lengths are given in centimetres.

(a) Show that it is not possible to sew this continuously without repeating any edges.

(b) State which edges have to be repeated.

(c) Hence find a possible route starting at A and finishing at A that covers every edge at least once.

3

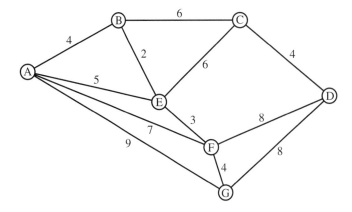

The network above shows the major roads that are to be gritted by a council in bad weather. The number on each arc is the length of the road in kilometres.

(a) List the valency of each of the vertices.

(b) Starting and finishing at A, use an algorithm to find a route of minimum length that covers each road at least once. State which (if any) roads will be traversed twice.

(c) Obtain the total length of your shortest route.

Test yourself

If your answer is incorrect:

1

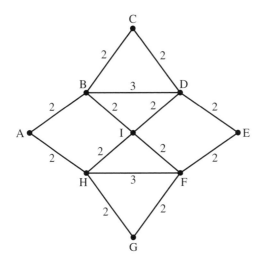

Review Heinemann Book D1 pages 91–96

The above pattern is to be machined onto a garment, starting and finishing at A. The machining is to be carried out continuously. Determine the total length of machining required, given that the lengths are given in inches. Write down a possible route.

2

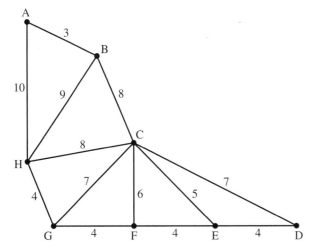

Review Heinemann Book D1 pages 91–96

For the above network find a minimum weight route starting and finishing at A and traversing every edge of the network at least once. Give its length.

Test yourself answers

1 Length = 30, ABCDBIDEFIHFGHA   **2** ABCDECEFCGFGHCBHA, length = 96

Critical path analysis

Key points to remember

In an activity network:

1 The **nodes** represent events.

2 The **arcs** represent activities.

3 The **weights** represent the duration of the corresponding activity.

4 The **source node** represents the beginning of the project.

5 The **sink node** represents the end of the project.

6 The **earliest time** e_i for node i is the earliest time we can arrive at event i.

7 The **latest time** l_i for node i is the latest time we can leave event i without extending the length of the critical path.

8 The **critical path** is the longest path through the network from the source node to the sink node.

9 Events i for which $e_i = l_i$ are **critical events**.

10 Activities (i, j) for which $l_j - e_i - [\text{duration } (i, j)] = 0$ are **critical activities**.

11 For activity (i, j) of duration a_{ij}:

> the earliest start time is e_i
> the earliest finish time is $e_i + a_{ij}$
> the latest finish time is l_j
> the latest start time is $l_j - a_{ij}$
> the total float on activity (i, j) is $l_j - e_i - a_{ij}$

Example 1

A company is about to introduce a new product (product 3). One unit of product 3 is produced by assembling one unit of product 1 and one unit of product 2. Before production begins on either product 1 or product 2 raw materials must be purchased and workers must be trained. Before products 1 and 2 can be assembled to produce product 3, product 2 must be inspected.

The table below gives a list of activities and their predecessors, and the duration of each activity.

Activity	Predecessor	Duration (days)
A (train workers)	—	6
B (purchase raw materials)	—	9
C (produce product 1)	A, B	8
D (produce product 2)	A, B	7
E (test product 2)	D	10
F (assemble products 1 and 2)	C, E	12

(a) Draw an activity network to show this information.
(b) Calculate the early and late times for each event.
(c) Hence determine the critical activities and the critical path. State the minimum time required to complete the project.
(d) Find the total float for each of the non-critical activities.
(e) Using the information obtained above draw a Gantt chart.

Answer

(a) The given information may be modelled by the network shown below.

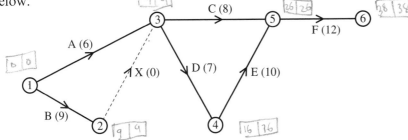

Notice that it is necessary to include a dummy activity X. This does, of course, have zero duration.

(b) The earliest and latest times for the events (nodes) are shown in the diagram below using the key

Earliest time	Latest time

Using 6 and 7

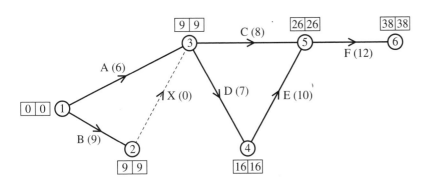

(c) Working backwards from ⑥ we can identify the **critical activities** as those with zero total float,
i.e. $l_j - e_i - [\text{duration } (i, j)] = 0$:

Using 10

$$\text{F: float} = 38 - 26 - 12 = 0$$
$$\text{E: float} = 26 - 16 - 10 = 0$$
$$\text{D: float} = 16 - 9 - 7 = 0$$
$$\text{X: float} = 9 - 9 - 0 = 0$$
$$\text{B: float} = 9 - 0 - 9 = 0$$

The **critical path** consists of activities B, X, D, E and F. Its length is the early start time of the end event ⑥ and is therefore 38 days.

Using 8

(d) The total floats of the non-critical activities are:

$$\text{A: } 9 - 0 - 6 = 3$$
$$\text{C: } 26 - 9 - 8 = 9$$

(e) The Gantt (cascade) chart shows all the above information with the critical activities on the first line and the non-critical activities A and C, with their floats of 3 and 9, on the second line.

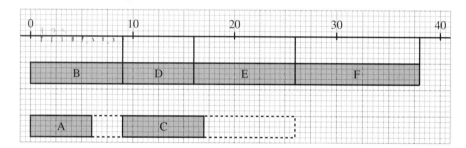

Revision exercise 5

1 Draw an activity network to represent the dependence table below, using a minimum number of dummies, given that the project is complete when all the activities are complete.

Activity	Depends on
A	—
B	—
C	—
D	A
E	B
F	B, C
G	A
H	D, E, F
I	G, H
J	G

2

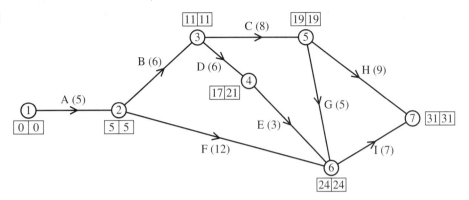

The diagram above shows an activity network that models a project. The durations of the activities A, B, C, ..., I are shown on the edges. Also shown are the early and late event

times in the form | Earliest time | Latest time |.

(a) Verify the early and late event times given on the diagram.

(b) Determine the critical activities and the length of the critical path.

(c) Obtain the total floats for the non-critical activities.

(d) On a grid draw a cascade (Gantt) chart showing the information found in parts (b) and (c).

Each activity requires one worker.

(e) Show that at least two workers will be required to complete the project in the critical time.

(f) Show that the project cannot be completed by two workers in the critical time. Explain your reasoning.

(g) Given that only two workers are available draw up a schedule to show how these should be allocated to complete the project in a minimum time. State this minimum time.

| **Test yourself** | **What to review** |

If your answer is incorrect:

1 A small building project is modelled by the activity network shown below. The number on each edge gives the duration of that activity in hours.

Review Heinemann Book D1 pages 114–126

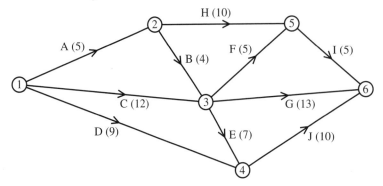

(a) Calculate the earliest and latest times for each event.

(b) Hence determine the critical activities and the critical path. State the minimum time required to complete the project.

(c) Find the total float for each of the non-critical activities.

(d) Using the information obtained above draw a Gantt chart for the project.

(e) Given that each activity requires one worker, show that at least three workers will be required to complete the project in the critical time.

(f) Draw up a schedule to show that the project can be completed by three workers in the critical time.

Test yourself answers

1 (a)

Event	1	2	3	4	5	6
Early time	0	5	12	19	17	29
Late time	0	8	12	19	24	29

(b) Critical activities: C, E and J.
Critical path: ① → ③ → ④ → ⑥
Minimum time 29 hr.

(c) Total floats:
A(3), B(3), D(10), F(7), G(4), H(9), I(7).

(d)

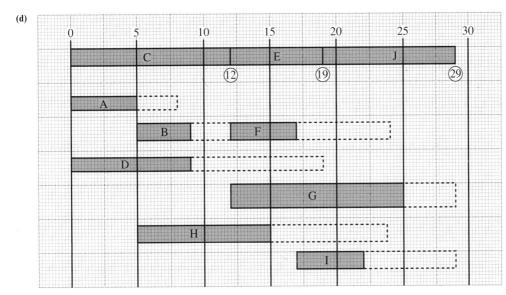

(e) Sum of lengths of activities is 80. $\dfrac{80}{29} = 2\dfrac{22}{29}$ ∴ at least 3.

(f)

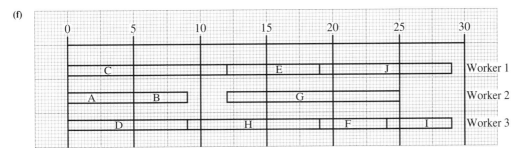

Linear programming

6

Key points to remember

1 Any pair of values of x and y that satisfy all the constraints in a linear programming problem is called a **feasible solution**.

2 The region that contains all feasible solutions is called the **feasible region**.

3 The **optimal solution** of a linear programming problem, if it exists, will occur at one or more of the extreme points (vertices) of the feasible region.

4 The **simplex method** is an algebraic method for solving linear programming problems.
  (i) The column that contains the entering variable is called the **pivotal column**.
  (ii) The row with the smallest θ value is called the **pivotal row**.
  (iii) The entry at the intersection of the pivotal row and the pivotal column is called the **pivot**.

5 **Optimality condition**
  If the objective row of a tableau has zero entries in the columns labelled by basic variables and no negative entries in the columns labelled by non-basic variables then the solution represented by the tableau is optimal.

Example 1

A jeweller makes bracelets and necklaces from gold and platinum. He has 18 ounces of gold and 20 ounces of platinum available. Each bracelet requires 2 ounces of gold and 4 ounces of platinum. Each necklace requires 3 ounces of gold and 2 ounces of platinum. A maximum of four bracelets can be sold. The sale of a bracelet makes £300 profit and the sale of a necklace makes £200 profit. The jeweller wishes to determine the number of bracelets and necklaces to make in order to maximise his profits. It may be assumed that all he makes can be sold.

(a) Formulate this as a linear programming problem.

(b) Solve the linear programming problem graphically.

Answer

Let x be the number of bracelets made and y be the number of necklaces made.
Then we have the following constraints:

gold: $\qquad\qquad\qquad 2x + 3y \leqslant 18$
platinum: $\qquad\qquad\quad 4x + 2y \leqslant 20$
number of bracelets: $\qquad x \leqslant 4$
non-negativity conditions: $\quad x \geqslant 0,\ y \geqslant 0$

Let the profit be £P, then:

$$P = 300x + 200y$$

The linear programming problem is then:
maximise $\qquad\qquad P = 300x + 200y$
subject to $\qquad\qquad\quad 2x + 3y \leqslant 18$
$\qquad\qquad\qquad\qquad 4x + 2y \leqslant 20$
$\qquad\qquad\qquad\qquad\quad\ \ x \leqslant 4$
$\qquad\qquad\qquad\ x \geqslant 0,\ y \geqslant 0$

(b) To obtain the feasible region we draw the lines:

l_1 – equation $2x + 3y = 18$ through $(0, 6)$ and $(9, 0)$
l_2 – equation $4x + 2y = 20$ through $(0, 10)$ and $(5, 0)$
l_3 – equation $x = 4$ through $(4, 0)$ and $(4, 8)$, for example

These are shown on the graph below together with the feasible region R, with vertices OABCD.

Using **2**

The feasible region is the unshaded region.

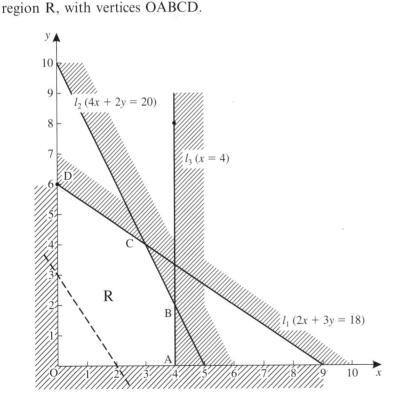

The coordinates of O, A and D can be written down immediately:
O is (0, 0) A is (4, 0) and D is (0, 6).
B is the point of intersection of $x = 4$ and $4x + 2y = 20$.
Substituting $x = 4$ in the second equation gives $y = 2$, so B is (4, 2).
C is the point of intersection of $4x + 2y = 20$ and $2x + 3y = 18$.
Multiplying the second equation by 2 gives $4x + 6y = 36$. Subtracting
the first equation gives $4y = 16$, $y = 4 \Rightarrow x = 3$, so C is (3, 4).
To find the optimal solution we can use either (i) the ruler method
or (ii) the vertex method.

Using **3**

Unless a particular method is specified, you may use either method
in the examination.
(i)   On the graph the profit line $300x + 200y = 600$ has been drawn
(the dotted line which passes through (0, 3) and (2, 0)).
Moving a ruler away from (0, 0) and parallel to this line identifies
C as the optimal point. At C(3, 4) the value of P is
$300(3) + 200(4) = 1700$, so the maximum profit is £1700 and is
achieved when the jeweller makes three bracelets and four necklaces.
(ii) To use the vertex method we must evaluate P at **all** the vertices
of the feasible region:

$$P_O = 300(0) + 200(0) = 0$$
$$P_A = 300(4) + 200(0) = 1200$$
$$P_B = 300(4) + 200(2) = 1600$$
$$P_C = 300(3) + 200(4) = 1700$$
$$P_D = 300(0) + 200(6) = 1200$$

The maximum value of P therefore occurs at C(3, 4) and is 1700. As
before therefore the maximum profit is £1700 and occurs when the
jeweller makes three bracelets and four necklaces.

Example 2
Use the simplex method to solve the linear programming problem:

maximize $\qquad P = 8x + 9y + 5z$

subject to $\qquad\qquad x + y + 2z \leqslant 2$
$$2x + 3y + 4z \leqslant 3$$
$$6x + 6y + 2z \leqslant 8$$
$$x \geqslant 0, y \geqslant 0, z \geqslant 0$$

Answer
We convert the inequalities to equalities by introducing slack
variables r, s and t, one in each of the first three constraints:

$$x + y + 2z + r = 2$$
$$2x + 3y + 4z + s = 3$$
$$6x + 6y + 2z + t = 8$$

$$x \geqslant 0, y \geqslant 0, z \geqslant 0, r \geqslant 0, s \geqslant 0, t \geqslant 0$$

The initial tableau is then:

Basic variable	x	y	z	r	s	t	Value	
r	1	1	2	1	0	0	2	
s	2	③	4	0	1	0	3	←
t	6	6	2	0	0	1	8	
P	−8	−9	−5	0	0	0	0	

↑

As (−9) is the most negative number in the bottom line the y column is the pivotal column.

Using **4** (i)

The θ values are:

$$\text{row } 1 = \tfrac{2}{1} = 2$$

$$\text{row } 2 = \tfrac{3}{3} = 1^*$$

$$\text{row } 3 = \tfrac{8}{6} = 1\tfrac{1}{3}$$

The pivotal row is therefore the second row and the pivot is 3 (as shown).

Using **4** (ii) and **4** (iii)

Dividing the pivotal row by 3 gives the new row 2

$$R_2': \quad \tfrac{2}{3} \quad 1 \quad \tfrac{4}{3} \quad 0 \quad \tfrac{1}{3} \quad 0 \quad | \quad 1$$

The second tableau is obtained by subtracting multiples of this row from the other rows to produce

$$\begin{array}{l} 0 \\ 1 \\ 0 \\ 0 \end{array} \text{ in the } y \text{ column.}$$

The second tableau is:

Basic variable	x	y	z	r	s	t	Value	
r	$\tfrac{1}{3}$	0	$\tfrac{2}{3}$	1	$-\tfrac{1}{3}$	0	1	$R_1 - R_2'$
y	$\tfrac{2}{3}$	1	$\tfrac{4}{3}$	0	$\tfrac{1}{3}$	0	1	
t	②	0	−6	0	−2	1	2 ←	$R_3 - 6R_2'$
P	−2	0	7	0	3	0	9	$R_4 + 9R_2'$

↑

The tableau is not optimal as there is a negative number (−2) in the bottom row. The pivotal column is now the x column.

The θ values are:

$$\text{row } 1 = \frac{1}{\left(\tfrac{1}{3}\right)} = 3$$

$$\text{row } 2 = \frac{1}{\left(\tfrac{2}{3}\right)} = \tfrac{3}{2} = 1\tfrac{1}{2}$$

$$\text{row } 3 = \tfrac{2}{2} = 1^*$$

So the pivotal row is the third row and the pivot is 2 (as shown). Dividing the pivotal row by 2 gives the new row 3

$$1 \quad 0 \quad -3 \quad 0 \quad -1 \quad \tfrac{1}{2} \quad | \quad 1$$

The third tableau is obtained by subtracting multiples of this row from the other rows to produce

$$\begin{matrix} 0 \\ 0 \\ 1 \\ 0 \end{matrix} \text{ in the } x \text{ column.}$$

The third tableau is:

Basic variable	x	y	z	r	s	t	Value
r	0	0	$\tfrac{5}{3}$	1	0	$-\tfrac{1}{6}$	$\tfrac{2}{3}$
y	0	1	$\tfrac{10}{3}$	0	1	$-\tfrac{1}{3}$	$\tfrac{1}{3}$
x	1	0	-3	0	-1	$\tfrac{1}{2}$	1
P	0	0	1	0	1	1	11

As there are no negative entries in the bottom row this is the optimal tableau. The optimal solution is $x = 1$, $y = \tfrac{1}{3}$, $z = 0$ and $P = 11$. The values of the slack variables are $r = \tfrac{2}{3}$, $s = 0$ and $t = 0$.

Using **5**

The objective function P has its maximum value of 11 when the variables have values $x = 1$, $y = \tfrac{1}{3}$ and $z = 0$. The values of the slack variables indicate:

$r = \tfrac{2}{3}$ – the first inequality is **not tight**. The left-hand side of the inequality is $\tfrac{2}{3}$ less than the right-hand side number 2

$s = 0$ – the second inequality is **tight**, that is the equality sign holds at the optimal values.

$t = 0$ – the third inequality is **tight**.

Revision exercise 6

1 Two bookcases, type A and type B, are manufactured in each of three departments, 1, 2 and 3. The table below shows the number of hours each type of bookcase spends in each department.

	A	B
Department 1	3	2
Department 2	1	4
Department 3	5	3

The total hours available in departments 1, 2 and 3 are 30, 40 and 35 respectively. When a bookcase of type A is sold a profit of £5 is made and when a bookcase of type B is sold a profit of £4 is made. The company wishes to maximise the profit made from the sale of bookcases.

Assuming all bookcases made can be sold, formulate the above situation as a linear programming problem.

2 Consider the linear programming problem:

maximise $\quad\quad P = 7x + 10y$

subject to $\quad\quad\quad 4x + 3y \leqslant 24$

$\quad\quad\quad\quad\quad\quad 2x + y \leqslant 10$

$\quad\quad\quad\quad\quad\quad\quad\quad y \leqslant 6$

$\quad\quad\quad\quad x \geqslant 0,\ y \geqslant 0$

(a) Find the feasible region for this problem.

(b) Use the vertex method to obtain the maximum value of P and the values of x and y for which this occurs.

3 A horticulturist needs to fertilise a plot ready for sowing a crop in the spring. Two fertilisers are available, 'Supergrow' and 'Plus'. A bag of 'Supergrow' provides 3 kg of nitrogen and 4 kg of phosphate. A bag of 'Plus' provides 4 kg of nitrogen and 2 kg of phosphate. The horticulturist requires at least 24 kg of nitrogen and at least 22 kg of phosphate. A bag of 'Supergrow' costs £5 and a bag of 'Plus' costs £4. The horticulturist wishes to determine how many bags of each fertiliser he needs to purchase in order to keep the cost of growing his crop to a minimum.

(a) Formulate this as a linear programming problem.

(b) Solve this linear programming problem graphically using the ruler method to find the optional solution.

4 Solve the linear programming problem below using the simplex algorithm:

maximise $\quad\quad P = x + 4y + 10z$

subject to $\quad\quad\quad x + 4y + 2z \leqslant 84$

$\quad\quad\quad\quad\quad\quad\quad x + 4z \leqslant 8$

$\quad\quad\quad\quad x \geqslant 0,\ y \geqslant 0,\ z \geqslant 0$

Test yourself	What to review

If your answer is incorrect:

1 A mining company has two mines, A and B. Mine A produces 2 tons of high-grade coal, 6 tons of medium-grade coal and 3 tons of low-grade coal each day. Mine B produces 4 tons of high-grade coal, 2 tons of medium-grade coal and 3 tons of low-grade coal each day.
To fulfill an order the company requires 160 tons of high-grade coal, 180 tons of medium-grade coal and 210 tons of low-grade coal. It costs the company £200 a day to operate mine A and £300 a day to operate mine B.
The company wishes to minimise the total cost of meeting this order and therefore wishes to know how many days it should operate mine A and how many days it should operate mine B.
Let x be the number of days A is operated and y be the number of days B is operated.
(a) Write down the inequalities satisfied by x and y.
(b) If £C is the cost of the operation, write down C in terms of x and y.
(c) Solve the resulting linear programming problem graphically to obtain the optimal values of x and y and the minimum value of C.

Review Heinemann Book D1 pages 134–157

2 Use the simplex algorithm to solve the linear programming problem:
maximize $P = 4x + 3y + 5z$
subject to $4x + 5y + 6z \leq 200$
$5y + 2z \leq 100$
$2x + y + z \leq 70$
$x \geq 0, y \geq 0, z \geq 0$

Review Heinemann Book D1 pages 166–175

Test yourself answers

1 **(a)** $2x + 4y \geq 160$, $6x + 2y \geq 180$, $3x + 3y \geq 210$ **(b)** $C = 200x + 300y$ **(c)** $x = 60$, $y = 10$, $C_{min} = £15\,000$
2 $x = 27\frac{1}{2}, y = 0, z = 15$, $P_{max} = 185$

Matchings

Key points to remember

1 A **bipartite graph** consists of two sets of vertices X and Y. The edges only join vertices in X to vertices in Y, not vertices within a set.

2 A **matching** in a bipartite graph is a subset M of the edges of the graph G such that no two edges in M have a common vertex.

3 A **maximum matching** M is a matching in which the number of edges is as large as possible.

The words *maximum* and *maximal* are effectively interchangeable.

4 In a bipartite graph with n vertices in each set a **complete matching** M is a matching in which the number of edges is also n.

5 An **alternating path** for a matching M in G is a path in G with the following properties:
 (i) it joins an unmatched vertex in X to an unmatched vertex in Y
 (ii) it is such that the edges in the path are alternatively **in** and **not in** the matching M.

6 **The matching improvement algorithm**
 Step 1 Start with any non-trivial matching M in G.
 Step 2 Search for an alternative path for M in G.
 Step 3 If an alternating path is found, construct a better matching M' by changing the status of the edges in the alternating path and return to step 2 with M' replacing M.
 Step 4 Stop when no alternating path can be found. The matching obtained is maximal.

Example 1

A Maths department has four teachers available: Miss Ahmed (A), Ms Brown (B), Mr Currie (C) and Dr Dougal (D). Four courses, pure maths (1), mechanics (2), statistics (3) and decision maths (4), have to be allocated, one to each teacher. The courses the teachers are willing to teach are shown below:

Miss Ahmed (A): any of the four courses
Ms Brown (B): pure maths, mechanics
Mr Currie (C): pure maths, statistics
Dr Dougal (D): pure maths

(a) Model this information with a bipartite graph.
(b) Miss Ahmed arrives first and claims pure maths. Then Mr Currie arrives and claims statistics. Show this initial matching in a distinctive way.
(c) Taking this matching as the initial matching, use the maximum matching algorithm to obtain a complete matching. State clearly the alternating paths you use.
(d) Explain why this is the only complete matching.

Answer

(a) The bipartite graph modelling the information given is:

Using **1**

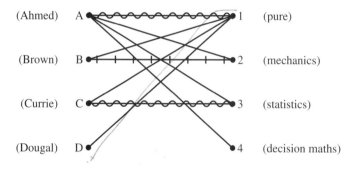

(b) The given initial matching is shown using ∿∿.

Using **2**

(c) To improve this initial matching we look for an alternating path. Starting with B, which is unmatched, we have the simple alternating path B———2. Changing status gives B∿∿2. This has been included in the diagram thus ┼┼┼.

Using **5**

The only remaining unmatched teacher is D.
Starting at D we have D———1∿∿A———4. Changing status gives D∿∿1———A∿∿4. The complete matching is then A(4), B(2), C(3), D(1).

Using **4**

(d) The only course D can teach is pure maths (1). The only teacher who is willing to teach decision maths (4) is teacher A. This leaves B and C to teach 2 and 3. Teacher B will not teach 3 (statistics) and Teacher C will not teach 2 (mechanics), and so the only possible match is B(2) and C(3). Therefore A(4), B(2), C(3), D(1) is the only complete matching.

Example 2

A company which sells china, plans to open four new shops in Bedford (B), Cambridge (C), Dunmow (D) and Ely (E). There are four managers available to manage these: Ms Richards (R), Miss Shore (S), Mr Trent (T) and Mrs Verity (V). The shops they are willing to manage are shown in the table below.

Ms Richards	Bedford, Ely
Miss Shore	Cambridge, Dunmow
Mr Trent	Ely
Mrs Verity	Ely, Bedford

(a) Show this information on a bipartite graph.
(b) Use the matching improvement algorithm to obtain a maximal matching and so decide if each manager will get a shop.

Answer

(a) The given information is summarised in the following bipartite graph:

Using

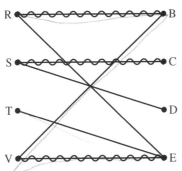

(b) Take as an initial matching R–B, S–C and V–E. This is shown on the diagram using ∿∿∿.

Using **2**

The only unmatched vertex in the left-hand set is T. Let us therefore try and find an alternating path starting at T:

Using **5**

$$T \text{——} E \text{∿∿} V \text{——} B \text{∿∿} R$$

As R is only joined to B and E, it is not possible to obtain an alternating path. Since no alternating path can be found, the matching above is a maximum matching. In this matching Mr Trent does not get a shop and the shop at Dunmow does not get a manager.

Using **3**

Revision exercise 7

1 Five boys, Bill (B), Gareth (G), Ian (I), Julian (J) and Peter (P), have been invited to lunch. Five packs of sandwiches have been ordered: cheese (C), ham (H), tuna (T), salmon (S) and egg (E). The boys were asked which sandwiches they did not like. Their answers are summarised in the table below.

	Cheese	Ham	Tuna	Salmon	Egg
Bill	X		X	X	
Gareth		X	X		X
Ian	X	X		X	
Julian	X			X	
Peter	X			X	X

(a) Produce a table that shows the sandwiches the boys do like.

(b) Show the information in the table produced in (a) on a bipartite graph.

(c) Use the maximum matching algorithm to obtain a maximum matching and hence determine whether or not it is possible to give each boy a packet of sandwiches he does like.

2 A garden centre has just opened a shop next to its plant area. It has hired five girls to work in the shop on Saturdays. The girls are Betty (B), Diane (D), Gillian (G), Mary (M) and Rachel (R). The departments in the shop are cards and pictures (1), books (2), indoor plants (3), fertilisers and insecticides (4), and pet foods (5). One girl is to be assigned to each department.

At their interview the girls were each asked which departments they would prefer to work in. The table below summarises their preferences.

Betty (B)	1, 4, 5
Diane (D)	3, 5, 1
Gillian (G)	2, 3
Mary (M)	1, 2, 3
Rachel (R)	2, 3

(a) Show this data on a bipartite graph.

(b) Initially the manager allocates Betty, Diane and Gillian to the first department in their lists. Show this initial matching in a distinctive way on the graph drawn in (a).

(c) Starting from this initial matching, use the maximum matching algorithm to obtain a complete matching. State clearly the alternating paths you use.

3

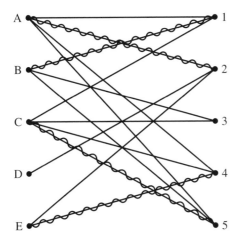

The above bipartite graph shows jobs 1, 2, 3, 4 and 5 and workers A, B, C, D and E. The arcs indicate which job a given worker is qualified to do. The arcs marked 〜〜〜 show an initial matching.

Obtain two alternating paths and hence obtain two complete matchings.

Test yourself	What to review

If your answer is incorrect:

1 Harry's Hardware has employed five new girls, Carol (C), Enid (E), Helen (H), Joan (J) and Norma (N), to work one in each of its five departments, garden supplies (G), screws and nails (S), kitchen utensils (K), paints (P) and tools (T). The girls were asked which departments they would prefer to work in and their answers are summarised in the table below.

Review Heinemann Book D1 pages 195–209

Carol	garden supplies, paints, screws and nails
Enid	tools, paints
Helen	kitchen utensils, garden supplies
Joan	screws and nails, paints
Norma	tools, kitchen utensils

(a) Show these preferences on a bipartite graph.
(b) Carol, Helen and Norma are allocated the first department in their list. Taking this matching as the initial matching, use the maximum matching algorithm to obtain a complete matching. State clearly the alternating paths you use.

(c) Norma says she would really like to sell kitchen utensils. If Norma is allowed to choose this department, determine whether or not it is possible to allocate all the other girls.

Test yourself answers

1 (a)

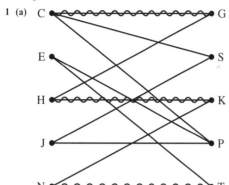

(b) Alternating paths e.g. J————P (breakthrough), E————P ∿∿∿ J————S (breakthrough)
Complete matching: (E and P), (J and S), (C and G), (H and K), (N and T).

(c) Yes. New complete matching is (N and K), (H and G), (C and S), (J and P), (E and T).

Flows in networks

8

8 The maximum flow algorithm is as follows:
Step 1 Obtain an initial flow by inspection.
Step 2 Find flow-augmenting paths using the labelling procedure until no further flow-augmenting paths can be found.
Step 3 Check that the flow obtained is maximal by finding a cut whose capacity is equal to the value of the flow.

9 A network with multiple sources $S_1, S_2, \ldots, S_m$ and multiple sinks $T_1, T_2, \ldots, T_n$ can be reduced to a network with only one source and one sink by introducing a **supersource** S and a **supersink** T. Arcs $SS_1, SS_2, \ldots, SS_m$ are added from the supersource S to the source $S_1, S_2, \ldots, S_m$. Arcs $T_1T, T_2T, \ldots, T_nT$ are added from sinks $T_1, T_2, \ldots, T_n$ to the supersink. The capacities of the new arcs can be considered to be infinite.

Example 1

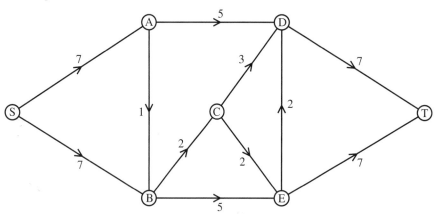

The above diagram shows a capacitated network. The number on each arc gives the capacity of that arc in appropriate units.
(a) State the maximum flow along:
(i) SBEDT
(ii) SBCDT.
(b) Taking your answer to (a) as the initial flow pattern, use the labelling procedure to find a maximum flow from S to T. List each flow-augmenting route you find together with its flow.
(c) Prove that your flow is maximal.

Answer

(a) The maximum flow along SBEDT is the minimum of the capacities of the arcs along this path, that is min $\{7, 5, 2, 7\} = 2$ units. Similarly, the maximum flow along SBCDT is min $\{7, 2, 3, 7\} = 2$ units.

Using

(b)

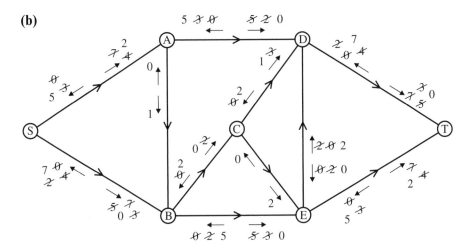

The two flows found in part (a) have been placed on the above figure as an initial flow pattern using the standard notation with forward and backward capacities.
Other flow-augmenting paths are:

Using **6**

> SADT (flow 3)
> SBET (flow 3)

These are also shown on the figure.
There is one other flow-augmenting path which is not quite so obvious as it uses a backflow on edge ED. This flow-augmenting path is **SADET** (flow 2). This is also shown on the figure.
The flow pattern is then:

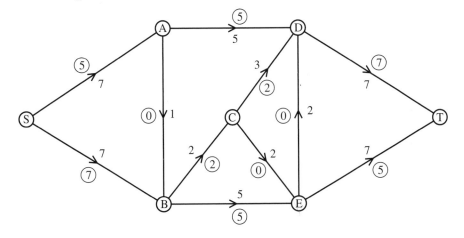

The total flow is 12 units.
(c) The flow is maximal since there is a cut of capacity 12, namely arcs AD, BC and BE.

Using **8**

Example 2

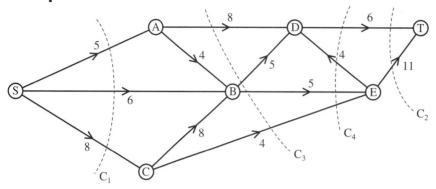

The above figure shows a capacitated network.
The number on each arc gives the capacity of that arc in appropriate units. Write down the capacity of the cuts C_1, C_2, C_3 and C_4. State the cut of minimum capacity. What can you deduce about the maximum flow from S to T?

Answer

$$C_1 = 5 + 6 + 8 = 19$$
$$C_2 = 11 + 6 = 17$$
$$C_3 = 8 + 5 + 5 + 4 = 22$$
$$C_4 = 4 + 5 + 6 = 15$$

The capacity of the minimum cut is 15.
This means that the maximum flow from S to T is 15 using:

$$\text{value of maximum flow} = \text{capacity of minimum cut}$$

Revision exercise 8

1

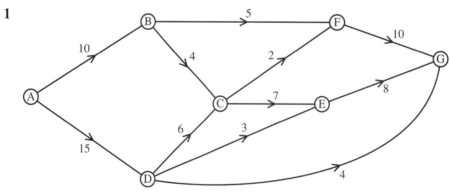

The diagram above shows a capacitated network.

(a) Find a maximal flow from A to G.

(b) Show your maximal flow on a diagram.

(c) Confirm that your flow is maximal by finding a minimum cut.

2

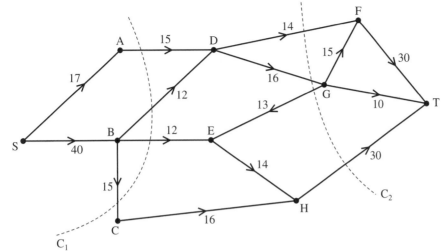

In the network above the number on each arc indicates the
maximum flow possible through that arc.

(a) Obtain the capacities of the cuts C_1 and C_2.

(b) Given that one of these cuts is a minimum cut, obtain the
maximum flow from the source S to the sink T.

(c) Hence obtain the flow along SA and SB in the maximum
flow pattern.

3

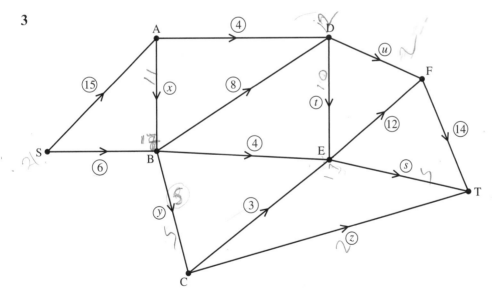

The figure above shows a capacitated network. The numbers
in rings are the flows along the edges in a given flow pattern.
Determine the values of x, y, z, s, t and u.

$y = 8 + 4 + 3 = 15$

$17 - 15 = 7$

4

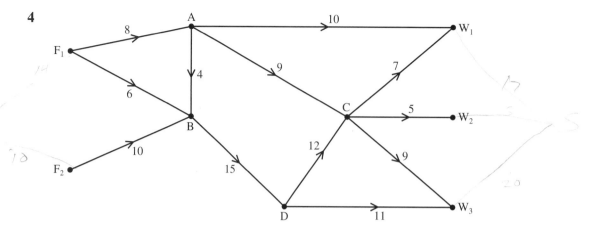

A manufacturing company has two factories, F_1 and F_2, and wishes to transport its products to three warehouses, W_1, W_2 and W_3. The capacities of the possible routes, in lorry loads per day, are shown in the figure above.

(a) Add a supersource F and a supersink W to obtain a single-source, single-sink capacitated network.

(b) Use the labelling procedure to obtain a maximal flow through the network. Show this flow pattern on a diagram.

(c) How many loads per day do W_1, W_2 and W_3 receive in this pattern?

Test yourself	**What to review**

If your answer is incorrect:

1 A gravel company has two plants, P_1 and P_2, and wishes to transport gravel to three sites, S_1, S_2 and S_3. The capacities of the possible routes, in truckloads per day, are shown in the figure below.

Review Heinemann Book D1(a) pages 234–236 (b) pages 221–232

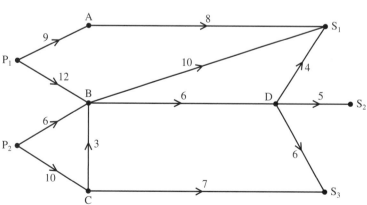

(a) Add a supersource P and a supersink S to obtain a single-source, single-sink capacitated network. State the capacities of the arcs you have added.

(b) Use the labelling procedure to obtain a maximal flow through the network. Show your flow pattern on a figure.

(c) Interpret your flow pattern giving:

    (i)   the number of truckloads leaving P_1 and P_2

    (ii) the number of truckloads reaching S_1, S_2 and S_3

    (iii) the number of truckloads passing through B each day.

Test yourself answers

1 (a)

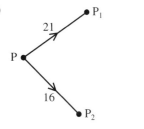 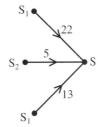

(b) Flows: e.g. PP_1 AS_1S (flow 8), PP_2 CS_3S (flow 7), PP_1 BS_1S (flow 10), PP_2 BDS_3S (flow 6)

This gives a maximal flow of 31. There is a cut consisting of arcs AS_1, BS_1, BD and CS_3 of capacity 31.

The flow pattern is

e.g.

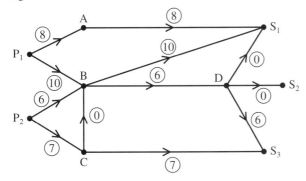

(c) (i) e.g. P_1: $8 + 10 = 18$, P_2: $6 + 7 = 13$ (ii) e.g. S_1: $8 + 10 + 0 = 18$, S_2: 0, S_3: $6 + 7 = 13$ (iii) Through B: $10 + 6 = 16$

Examination style paper

Attempt **all** questions.   **Time 90 minutes**

1

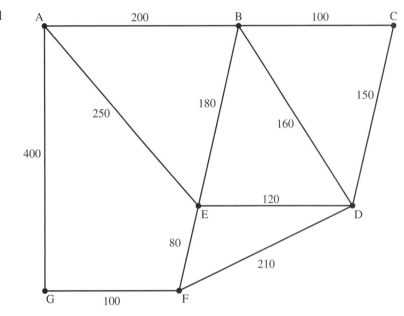

The diagram shows the network of roads on a new estate. The numbers indicate the length of the roads, in metres. The local council have a depot at C. To check on the street lighting they wish to start from C, travel along each road at least once, and return to C, whilst travelling a minimum distance. Use an appropriate algorithm to obtain a suitable route. Give the total length of this route.   **(7 marks)**

2   Five people 1, 2, 3, 4, 5 are being considered for five jobs A, B, C, D and E. The jobs they are qualified for are shown in the bipartite graph below.

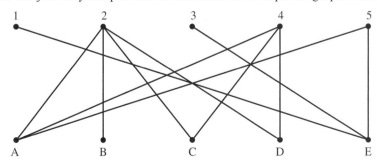

An initial matching M is made of 5 with E and 4 with D.

(a) Write down two alternating paths for M in G, one starting at 1 and the other starting at 2. **(3 marks)**

(b) Use these paths, in turn, to produce an improved matching with 4 edges. **(3 marks)**

(c) Given a reason why this matching is a maximal matching.

(2 marks)

3 A sixth form college wishes to network its six computers situated in blocks A, B, C, D, E and F. Cables need to be laid to link the computers.. As cable laying is expensive they wish to use a minimum total length of cable. The table below shows the shortest distance, in metres, between the various blocks.

	A	B	C	D	E	F
A	—	100	95	85	250	80
B	100	—	70	105	150	60
C	95	70	—	55	160	120
D	85	105	55	—	210	130
E	250	150	160	210	—	200
F	80	60	120	130	200	—

(a) Use Prim's algorithm to obtain a minimum connector and hence find the minimum total length of cable required. You should indicate clearly the order in which the arcs are selected in your minimum connector. **(5 marks)**

The principal decides the computer in block C will not be networked.

(b) Find the minimum length of cable required to link the remaining computers. **(3 marks)**

4 (a) Describe briefly the first-fit decreasing algorithm for bin packing. **(2 marks)**

A small building project is to be completed in 15 days. The jobs involved in the project and their durations, in days, are given in the table below. Each job requires one worker.

A	B	C	D	E	F	G	H	I
8	7	2	3	10	4	3	2	6

(b) Show that at least 3 workers will be required. **(1 mark)**

(c) Carry out the algorithm you have described in (a). **(3 marks)**

(d) Decide if it is possible to complete the project with only 3 workers in the given time. Explain your reasoning. **(4 marks)**

5 The figure shows a capacitated, directed network. The number on each arc indicates the capacity of that arc.

(a) State the maximum flow along (i) SABT, (ii) SADCT. **(2 marks)**

(b) Show these maximum flows on a copy of the figure.

(1 mark)

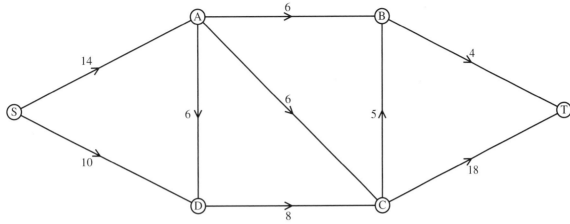

(c) Taking your answer to (b) as the initial flow pattern use the labelling algorithm to find a maximum flow from S to T. State your flow-augmenting paths. **(6 marks)**

(d) Prove that your flow is maximal. **(2 marks)**

6 The following linear programming problem arose during the course of an investigation.

Maximise $\qquad P = 16x + 20y + 10z$

subject to $\qquad 4x + 4y + z \leqslant 100$

$\qquad\qquad 5x + 2y + z \leqslant 80$

$\qquad\qquad x \geqslant 0,\ y \geqslant 0,\ z \geqslant 0$

The simplex algorithm is to be used to solve this problem.

(a) Write down the initial tableau using r and s as slack variables. **(3 marks)**

(b) Use the simplex algorithm to solve the problem giving the maximum value of P and the values of x, y and z for which it occurs. **(9 marks)**

7

Activity	Depends on
A	—
B	—
C	A
D	A
E	A, B
F	C
G	C, D, E
H	F, G

The dependence table for the activities involved in the first stage of a building project is shown above.

(a) Draw an activity network to show this information. **(3 marks)**

(b) Explain why it is necessary to add some dummies when drawing this activity network. **(2 marks)**

The second, independent stage of the project is represented by the activity network below. The numbers in brackets indicate the time in days to complete each activity.

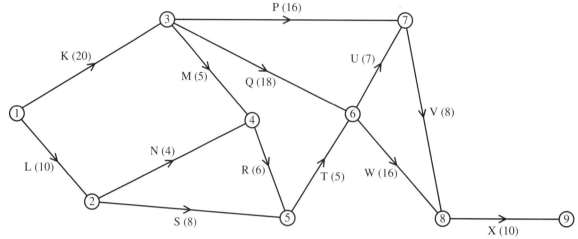

(c) Calculate the earliest time and the latest time for each event and enter them in boxes at each event thus:

Earliest time	Latest time

(6 marks)

(d) Hence determine the critical path and the length of the critical path. **(2 marks)**

Each activity requires one worker.

(e) Show that at least 3 workers will be required to complete the project in the critical time. **(2 marks)**

(f) Display the activities on a timeline with all activities starting as soon as possible and hence show that the project can be completed by 3 workers in the critical time. **(4 marks)**

Answers

Revision exercise 1

1 9

2 $x = 3$, $y = 2$

3 24, 30, 38, 46, 57, 63

4 **(a)** 4 **(b)** 3

5 6 LION

Revision exercise 2

1 A 4 B 1 D 2 C 3 A

2

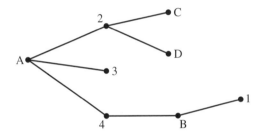

3

	A	B	C	D	E	F
A	0	15	—	—	10	20
B	15	0	12	—	8	—
C	—	12	0	11	15	—
D	—	—	11	0	25	22
E	10	8	15	25	0	7
F	20	—	—	22	7	0

4 ABE, ACBE, ACE, ADE, ACDE

5 No. There are four odd vertices, A, D, 2 and 4. We can only draw a Eulerian cycle when all vertices are even.

6 Add the edge AC. This makes the vertices A and C even – they were originally odd. All vertices are now even and so the graph has a Eulerian cycle:

e.g. ACDECBEFGEAGBA

Revision exercise 3

1

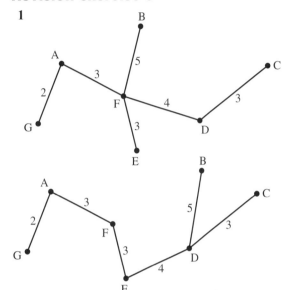

Total weight $= 2 + 3 + 3 + 3 + 4 + 5 = 20$

2

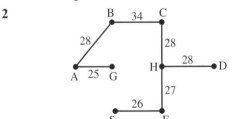

196 metres

3 e.g.

	1	2	7	4	3	6	5
	A	**B**	**C**	**D**	**E**	**F**	**G**
A		10	12	23			
B	⑩			18	12		
C	12			12		⑧	
D	23	18	12		⑩	10	9
E		⑫		10			13
F			8	⑩			14
G				⑨	13	14	

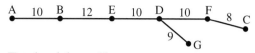

Total weight = 59

4 (a)

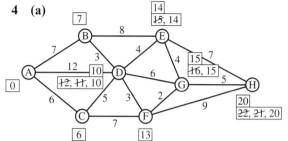

Shortest route is ACFGH,
length = 20 miles

(b) Shortest route is ABDEH,
length = 21 miles

5 A Hamiltonian circuit is ABDECA

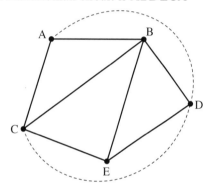

Revision exercise 4

1 (a) The valencies of the vertices are all even
and so the graph is traversable.

(b) A possible route is ABCDADCBA,
length = 126.

2 (a) The valencies of the vertices are A (2),
B (3), C (1), D (2), E (2), F (2), G (4).
As some vertices are odd it is not possible to
sew this continually without repeating edges.

(b) The edges to be repeated are those on
the path joining the odd vertices B and C,
namely BD and DC.

(c) A possible route is AGBDCDBEGFA,
length = 54 + 18 = 72.

3 (a) A (4), B (3), C (3), D (3), E (4), F (4), G (3)

(b) BE, EF, FG and CD will be traversed twice.

A possible route is ABCDGFDCEFGAFEBEA

(c) Minimum length = 66 + 13 = 79

Revision exercise 5

1

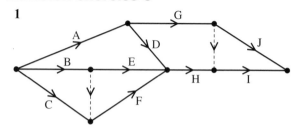

2 (b) Critical activities: A, B, C, G, I
Length of critical path = 31

(c) Total floats: D (4), E (4), F (7), H (3)

(d)

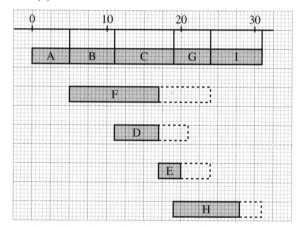

(e) Total weight of edges = 61

$$\frac{\text{total weight}}{\text{critical time}} = \frac{61}{31} = 1\frac{30}{31}$$

So more than one worker is required, that is
at least two workers are required.

(f) One worker can complete the critical
activities in the critical time. The non-critical
activities have a total weight of
$6 + 3 + 12 + 9 = 30$. However, none of these
can start until A is complete, that is after 5
(event 2). The project therefore cannot be
completed by two workers in the critical time.

(g) Note the following:
A to G as before. F can start any time after A
is complete (5). D can start any time after
B (11) is complete. E can start any after D (17).

Event ⑥ will then have an early time of 26 if F, D, E are scheduled for worker 2 as shown. Then H may be done by worker 1 and I by worker 2. Both workers will finish at 33. The minimum time required to complete the project with two workers is 33.

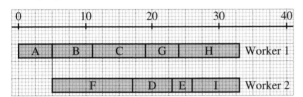

Revision exercise 6

1 x = number of A made

   y = number of B made

   Profit = £P

   Maximise $\qquad P = 5x + 4y$

   subject to $\qquad 3x + 2y \leqslant 30$

   $\qquad\qquad\qquad x + 4y \leqslant 40$

   $\qquad\qquad\qquad 5x + 3y \leqslant 35$

2 **(b)** The vertices of the feasible region are O (0, 0), A (5, 0), B (3, 4), C ($1\frac{1}{2}$, 6) and D (0, 6).

   $P_O = 0$, $P_A = 35$, $P_B = 61$, $P_C = 70\frac{1}{2}$, $P_D = 60$

   Maximum P of value $70\frac{1}{2}$ occurs at C, $x = 1\frac{1}{2}$, $y = 6$

3 **(a)** Minimise $\qquad C = 5x + 4y$

   subject to $\qquad 3x + 4y \geqslant 24$

   $\qquad\qquad\qquad 4x + 2y \geqslant 22$

   $\qquad\qquad\qquad x \geqslant 0, y \geqslant 0$

   (b) $x = 4$, $y = 3$, $C = 32$

4 $x = 0$, $y = 20$, $z = 2$ $\quad P_{max} = 100$

Revision exercise 7

1

	C	H	T	S	E
B		✓			✓
G	✓			✓	
I			✓		✓
J		✓	✓		✓
P		✓	✓		

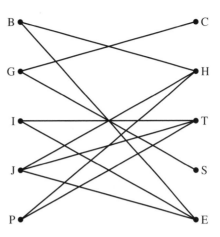

A maximal matching is (B–H), (G–C) (I–T), (J–E). Taking this as the initial matching it is not possible to find an alternating path and hence it is maximal. It is therefore not possible to give each boy a pack of sandwiches he likes.

2 **(a)** and **(b)**

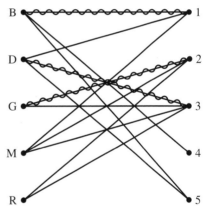

Use alternating paths

e.g. $\qquad$ M—1 〜〜〜 B—4

and

$\qquad\qquad$ R—3 〜〜〜 D—5

The complete matching then obtained is e.g.

(M 〜〜〜 1), (B 〜〜〜 4), (R 〜〜〜 3), (D 〜〜〜 5) and (G 〜〜〜 2)

3 Two of (i) D—2 〜〜〜 A—1 〜〜〜 B—3

   Changing status

   D 〜〜〜 2—A 〜〜〜 1—B 〜〜〜 3

   Complete matching:

   (A 〜〜〜 1) (B 〜〜〜 3) (C 〜〜〜 5) (D 〜〜〜 2) (E 〜〜〜 4)

(ii) D—2 ∿∿∿ A—5 ∿∿∿ C—3

Changing status

D ∿∿∿ 2—A ∿∿∿ 5—C ∿∿∿ 3

Complete matching:

(A ∿∿∿ 5) (B ∿∿∿ 1) (C ∿∿∿ 3)

(D ∿∿∿ 2) (E ∿∿∿ 4)

(iii) D—2 ∿∿∿ A—1 ∿∿∿ B—5 ∿∿∿ C—3

Changing status

D ∿∿∿ 2—A ∿∿∿ 1—B ∿∿∿ 5—C ∿∿∿ 3

Complete matching:

(A ∿∿∿ 1) (B ∿∿∿ 5) (C ∿∿∿ 3)

(D ∿∿∿ 2) (E ∿∿∿ 4)

Revision exercise 8

1 (a) Maximal flow is 19

   (b) A maximal flow pattern is

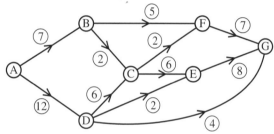

   (c) The minimum cut consists of arcs BF, CF, EG and DG, capacity $5 + 2 + 8 + 4 = 19$.

2 (a) The capacity of C_1 is the sum of the capacities of AD, BD, BE and BC
   $= 15 + 12 + 12 + 15 = 54$.

   The capacity of C_2 is the sum of capacities of DF, DG and HT (not EG)
   $= 14 + 16 + 30 = 60$

   (b) Since the value of maximum flow = capacity of minimum cut, the value of maximum flow is 54 units.

   (c) The flow along SA must be the same as the flow along AD, which is saturated, i.e. 15 units.

   The flow along SB must be the sum of the flows along BD, BE and BC, which are all saturated, i.e. $12 + 12 + 15 = 39$ units

3 $x = 11$, $y = 5$, $z = 2$, $s = 5$, $t = 10$, $u = 2$

4 (a)

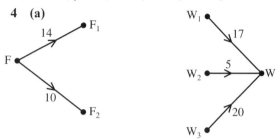

   (b) The maximum flow through the network is 23 units. This is a maximum as there is a cut of capacity 23 comprising (e.g.) the arcs F_1A and BD $(8 + 15)$. A flow pattern is

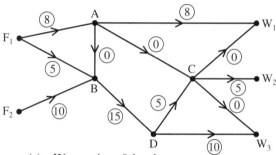

   (c) W_1 receives 8 loads
   W_2 receives 5 loads
   W_3 receives 10 loads

Examination style paper

1 The algorithm to be used is the chinese postman algorithm.

   A suitable route is CDBEDFEAGFEABC

   Total length of route 2280 metres.

2 (a) $1 - E = 5 - A$; $2 - D = 4 - C$.

   (b) (1, E), (2, D), (4, C), (5, A).

   (c) The only job 1 and 3 are qualified for is E. So one will be unmatched.

   Jobs A, C, D can only be done by two people 2 and 4. So one job will not get done.

3 (a) Minimum connector

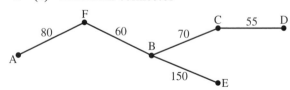

   Edges added in order AF, FB, BC, CD, BE.

   Total length of cable is 415 metres.

(b) Now minimum connector is

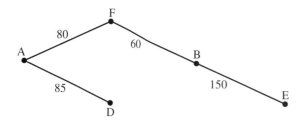

Total length 375 metres.

4 (a) Sort the jobs according to their duration with longest first. Construct bins of given size and fit a job into the first bin which has sufficient spare capacity.

(b) Total of durations
$8 + 7 + 2 + 3 + 10 + 4 + 3 + 2 + 6 = 45$
$\frac{45}{15} = 3$ ∴ at least 3 workers

(c) Order jobs: E(10), A(8), B(7), I(6), F(4), D(3), G(3), C(2), H(2)

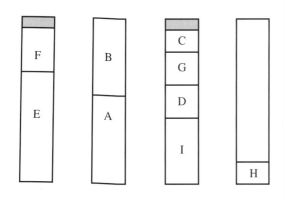

(d) Yes it is possible using full bin combinations. Full bins A and B; E, C and D; I, G, F and H.

5 (a) (i) max flow along SABT is 4 units
(ii) max flow along SADCT is 6 units.

(b)

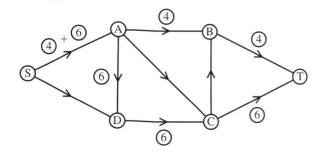

(c) Flow-augmenting paths
e.g. SDCT – 2 units
SDACT – 6 units
Maximum flow – 18 units

(d) There is a cut comprising the arcs DC, AC and BT of capacity 18 units. Maximal by maximum flow – minimum cut theorem.

6 (a)

Basic variable	x	y	z	r	s	Value
r	4	4	1	1	0	100
s	5	2	1	0	1	80
P	−16	−20	−10	0	0	0

(b) $x = 0$, $y = 10$, $z = 60$
$P_{max} = 800$

7 (a)

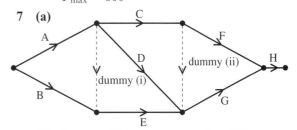

(b) Dummy (i) is necessary as C and D depend only on A but E depends on A and B.
Dummy (ii) is necessary as F depends only on C but G depends on C and *also* on D and E.

(c) ① $\boxed{0\,|\,0}$, ② $\boxed{10\,|\,25}$, ③ $\boxed{20\,|\,20}$,
④ $\boxed{25\,|\,27}$, ⑤ $\boxed{31\,|\,33}$, ⑥ $\boxed{38\,|\,38}$,
⑦ $\boxed{45\,|\,46}$, ⑧ $\boxed{54\,|\,54}$, ⑨ $\boxed{64\,|\,64}$,

(d) Critical activities: K(20), Q(18), W(16) and X(10)
Length of critical path is 64 days.

(e) Sum of duration of activities is 133 days.
$\frac{133}{64} = 2\frac{5}{64}$. At least 3 workers are required.

(f)

Heinemann Modular Mathematics for Edexcel AS and A Level

The leading course for Edexcel A Level

Heinemann Modular Mathematics for **Edexcel AS and A Level** provides dedicated syllabus-specific textbooks to give you a clear route to success. The clear layout and structure of the books match the flexible modular structure of the course, meaning that you only study the elements you need to. Perfect for use in the classroom or at home, the series covers the topics at the level and depth that you'll need. Each book includes lots of test questions and answers, and features a full mock-exam paper.

All the books have been written by experienced teachers who have been involved with the development of the new specification, so you can be sure that these are the right textbooks for you.

To see any of the following titles FREE for 60 days or to order your books straight away call Customer Services on 01865 888068

Pure Mathematics 1 (P1)
0434 510886

Pure Mathematics 2 (P2)
0435 510894

Pure Mathematics 3 (P3)
0435 510908

Pure Mathematics 4 (P4)
0435 510916

Pure Mathematics 5 (P5)
0435 510924

Pure Mathematics 6 (P6)
0435 510932

Mechanics 1 (M1)
0435 510746

Mechanics 2 (M2)
0435 510754

Mechanics 3 (M3)
0434 510762

Mechanics 4 (M4)
0435 510770

Mechanics 5 (M5)
0435 510789

Mechanics 6 (M6)
0435 510797

Statistics 1 (S1)
0435 510827

Statistics 2 (S2)
0435 510835

Statistics 3 (S3)
0435 510843

Statistics 4 (S4)
0435 510851

Statistics 5 (S5)
0435 51086X

Statistics 6 (S6)
0435 510878

Decision Mathematics (D1)
0435 510800

Decision Mathematics (D2)
0435 510819

S 999 ADV 08